Watchmen

Brian Ingemann Schierning Holme

Collection of poems & poetry

Watchmen

The BoD Publishing house

2020 © Brian Ingemann Schierning Holme
Book cover: Brian Ingemann Schierning Holme
The book is written in Times New Roman & Lucida Calligraphy
Publisher: BoD – Hellerup, Denmark
Printing: BoD – Norderstedt, Germany
ISBN: 978-87-4302-962-5

www.bod.dk
www.BrianISHolme@gmail.com

table of contents

Bonus!!!

Preface

Where do you go when the world collapses and
how did you even get back on top, where did you
get the energy to become a part of society once
more, where did the pain vanish to.

In a society where stress, depression and confusion
often lay a man down, you do not notice that little
thing that got you back on track. That one person
that miraculously entered your life briefly and
pulled you back towards life. The one person that
lives his entire life anonymous and faceless.

This collection of poems is the portrait of one of
those persons. We are many born with
unconditional empathy.

Omnes conjuncti sumus. (We are all connected)

I will end the preface with this passage.

Love gives the strength to see beyond.
Use the strength to see others and help.

Pleasant reading

Brian Ingemann Schierning Holme

Poems

Attractions

Worthy is the human
Who treasures all life
Who nourishes it
And lets it grow

Worthy is the man
Who loves a woman whole
Who respects and honours her
And lets her blossom

Worthy is the woman
Who loves a man whole
Who respects and cares for him
And lets him grow within

Whether you are man or woman
Always be true to each other
We cannot survive without each other
That is why love is bliss.

Conceived

A heart filled with light
A mind filled with darkness
A walk in the shadow of loneliness
A punishment fitting the crime.

Born with the ability to see beyond
Closing it, denying it, rejecting it
Never looking, never using, I will not
Living in the loneliness of emotional solitude.

A prisoner in time and knowledge
A misunderstood schizoid time traveler
Did not see the dark awakening
The seduction of the flesh.

Walking in this world alone
Hoping someone will see
What lies beyond the flesh
The passion that lies in me.

In the meadows

Running through the meadows
Blue sky of happiness
Butterflies painting colors
Flowers scenting enchanted

Lying in the meadows
Watching clouds forming
Feeling butterflies tickling
Scenting the pillow of flowers

Happy thoughts in my head
Happy emotions in my heart
Sizzling feeling in my body
Scenting state of euphuism

A product of love
Giving love to the world
Energetic instrument
Seeing with eyes of love

Nexus

Naive is the soul that is pure
Pure is the soul that is untouched
Untouched is the soul that has never seen
Never seen has the soul that is naive

In the soul that is pure lies love
In the soul that is untouched lies goodness
In the soul that has never seen lies kindness
In the soul that is naive lies forgiveness

Beauty sparks in a soul that is fair
A soul like that is very rare
Souls are often touched and impure
But occasionally a soul is to endure

To find a soul in which virtues are honorable
Is a search in which no hope lies beyond
But seeing into a soul like that
Is a moment in time standing still

The voice of the past

Alarm clock is shouting
A new morning has arisen
Horizon greats with red dawn
Giving nourishment to the soul

The smell of fresh brewed coffee
Bewilders my sense of smell
Philosophical state of body
Do not know what the day will bring

Walking through the streets of emotions
Letting my soul run free to feel
Impressions bombarding with energies
Loving the complexity of people

Walking among the humans
As an entity without an equal
Helping the needed from within
Never wanting anything in return

Crack

Whispers loudly scream
Sadness silently kills inside
Loneliness turns into solitude
Sociality is but a distant roar

The horrible truth of life
Love is but an emotion
Built upon the vast nothingness
A monolith for a shred for hope to cling unto

The ill faith is bestowed the human
Who tears down the walls of indifference?
Simply to watch them re-emerge again
A task entrusted a guardian of life

Transcripts of time rebuilding inside
A vortex wave of beguiled destruction
No hope, no faith, no love, no future
Waiting for inevitability to reclaim

Purity

Love is a sacred bond,
A bond between two souls,
A gesture of acceptance,
Giving your true inner self.

Combining getting stronger,
Stronger as a unity that knows,
The ways of the other heart,
Feeling with the selective soul.

Ups and downs are unavoidable,
It is how they are handled,
Fighting with the selective soul,
Is the way that it might work.

As long as the souls are pure,
A love will always be strong,
But if the soul breaks, and is defiled,
Then the chance of love surviving is slim.

Relic

Expiring oldish dying breed
a kind heart for help in need
different the persons the same ideals
a rare phenomenon in these times

Ideals which once were codes
now just a sigh in the wind
a vague instinctive remembrance
for many a time-consuming gesture

A breed the last generation of distinquisness
gentlemen in time and tide
always before now and after
the instinct will remain inside

To be a part of a breed like that
is the greatest honor to ever have
an honorable salute to an era gone
a proud hope it will blossom again

The lady knight

A lady of honor and time
Strong willed mind a fighter for love
Virtues respected and real
A lady of gold knows to feel

Treated equal to man or woman
Disrespect is a crime in heart
To a lady like in her status
Turning her back in punishment

Treated with honor and respect
She will be at your side
A friend in need and time
She will fight for you side by side

She is the female knight
Who aids people in despair?
She will do whatever it takes
For the knight's codex is her way

New beginning

Twilight colored skyline
Dark clouds hovering above
Fresh moist hanging in the air
Sensing the forthcoming of rain

The sky opens up in all its might
The soothing sound of rain on the window
The comfort emotion of new freshness
The inner warmth of touching waters

Running in the rain letting it caress
Beauty in the flexibility of the rain
The duality of contact with the ground
The bodily sense emotions of fresh wetness

Rain stops twilight fades away
The emerging scent of fresh grass
Magical enchantment of rainbow colors
Enjoying each second as an eternal expression

The muse

A maiden so pretty and fair
Bright shining eyes full of life
A voice as sweet as a summer breeze
A heart as large as the sun

A muse for inspiration of life
A talisman for a brighter day
A refreshing warmth as the summer dew
A kind, compassionate and caring maiden

Surrounded by an oral of light
Enchanting everyone she encounters
Giving them a piece of her heart
Letting them see the beauty of life

She gives without wanting
She is the instrument of joy
The way towards happiness
Of a maiden a muse in time

The power within

When love finds the power
The power to prevail
Then the fight has just begun
And there forever after lies hope

The hope that love will conquer
All the flaws and despairs
To enter the stage after the fight
As a whole unity of might

Kingdoms will come, and kingdoms will fall
But never forget the love for all
Fight for love fight with love
Then you will always rise above

In this world and in our little time
Love is the passion that keeps us alive
That keeps us going even when all is lost
Keep the love, the faith, and the trust

Tormented

Heartbeats divided in time
Fighting emotions splitting in two
Mind in heart battling in love's name
Beauty feeding the power to do so

Two worlds divided by experienced beliefs
Internal conflict soaring in my head
My heart has found a way through the dark
My mind reminding me, the difference

Every day you light my presence
With your prettiness and your smiling eyes
Showing me, confusing me, testing me
Madness in the name of all that is holy

Knowing that I would never accept
Feeling that I would crack by your touch
Wanting to escape into your embracing arms
Needing to feel the love inside of me

Shop of philosophy

Everybody wants to be in the present
The present is too late
The present has been there
The present has already become the future

Here is the new present
The new present is already too late
The new present has already been here
The new present has already become the new future

The future has once been the present
The present will always become the future
The future is often lived in the present
The present is often postponed to the future

Many people have the ability
To choose the present or future that discard
responsibility
But always choose the present
That makes you a better person in the future

Artefact

Chronicles of nothingness
mortal manifests
used temptations
fortified actions.

Everyone takes action
no one takes consequence
humanness is dying
fighting to prevail it.

Losing a battle
that is unwinnable
hate for love and life
insanity building up.

Sweet addiction
fading away from the world
floating in nothingness
waiting for resurrection.

Breaking points

When you are confided in love,
and love is confided in you,
then you are seriously trapped,
and there is absolutely nothing you can do.

When you do not know where hope is gone,
and you have gone without hope,
and you have gone in search of hope,
then there is no hope at all.

Soberness is the suffering condition,
between drunkenness,
drunkenness is the forgetting point,
between soberness.

Busstop to nowhere

When love is tom,
I see a fight for sanity.
Losing battle,
repenting love.
Tearing apart the reality.
Floating into spacelesness,
hovering above the mind that used to be.
Waiting, expecting, wanting, needing, demanding.
Everlasting emptiness in progress.
Wondering what went wrong.
Searching where did I go,
feeling a shredded unreal hope.
Lying beneath in remorse,
roaming the shadows of darkness.
Waiting for the impact to occur,
the impact of the battle between sanity and
insanity.
Spirits roaming, floating in my empty shell,
wanting, waiting fighting to take their place.
What do we do, where do we go, how can we
prevent?
Entering the light, I see a clouded mind fleeing in
sanity,
rejected by the mind of insanity,
rebirth is in progressive stage,
I cannot hold on much longer, I fight,
fight for the right to keep my sanity.
I can feel I am losing the battle.
Will I wander in nothingness always?
Or will I survive.
Am I to become a memory that fades away?
Nearly to be a vague remembrance.

Fascination

Chitchat laughing humming stories
Happy people busy people
Filled rooms individuals multiple
People coming and going constant impressions

Sense impressions in constant motion
Sitting still and enjoying the presence
The observers prerogative warming
Humans in all its glory and delight

Boys, girls, old, young and all other shapes
Sitting undisturbed and enjoying moments
Some gesticulate and hum to each other
Others babble on and laugh together

The uncomplexed relationship of just being
A common voice split in symmetric tones
Room filled with warmth and intensity
The charming face of all

Cardboard cases

Hollow is the man.
Who had everything,
yet had nothing.
Who lost everything,
yet lost nothing.

Numb less is the man.
Who walked off his own path,
to find out where he was going.
Simply just to find out,
he was still walking his own path.

Dreamless is the man.
Who knew his own demise?
That the ability he was born with,
was absorbing everybody's demises
unable ever to rise above them.

Empty is the man.
Who is hollow inside,
who is numb less in mind,
who is dreamless in life?
then love becomes nothingness.

Faces

Trapped within my own perimeter
the little boy inside is gone
darkness is cloaking the way out
My will to spring free is fading.

Looking into the mirror
my face is slowly changing
forming to the darkness that lies inside
nothing I do can prevent it.

The man inside
is seduced by the darkness
embracing it with his tormented life
forgetting his essence of the boy.

Walking in the streets
darkness puts on a happy face
but inside he is winning the battle
the little boy will never prevail.

Balled of the virgin paradox

Breathtaking beauty
Children of Aphrodite
Swaying hypnotically
Hearts desire warming

Gentle touch
Confirming affection
Soft voices
Whispering in loves name

Radiant daring eyes
Describing intentions
Twisting desires luring
Silent sighs demanding

Intertwining bodies toying
Unconditional presence soar
Persevering inner glows on fire
Mutual respect acknowledges

Ipso Facto

I'm wondering restlessly in despair,
not knowing where I'm going,
or even where I've been,
black darkness consuming,
changing the very essence of me,
bewildering I let it do so.

Inspiration gone no sources left,
everything has gone wrong and always has,
only two things repeat in my mind,
hate for life, hate for time,
good must be the devil's instrument,
and evil the instrument of god.

In my heart nothing remains,
except the aching and the pain,
I will wonder always still,
never able to stop and feel,
the world is not my space,
I am an alien in this place.

Impressions

Children playing together
The sweet sound of innocence
Parental emotions of pleasure
Pleasure for their children's happiness

Noticing the young lady across
She is viewing me curiously
She sees me seeing her and smiles to me
I smile back with an acknowledging smile

Interrupted by a loud echoing Hello
I greet back and we chitchat a while
An old friend from before time of times
The joy of reunion is well deserved

A young couple is sitting and giggling
Love is shining brightly from them
Their happiness is warming my heart
A sensuous warmth of just being

All these daily impressions
Makes my coffee heavenly good

Outer perimeter

Betrayed by the ones you love,
torn apart in a moment's insanity,
loving every minute.
Facing death repeatedly,
becoming a habit,
dying is a reward for the living who dares.
Facing the devil so many times, never loosing,
human strength in gathering, for the final task.
I will dance with the devil,
and I will lead a victorious crusade.
A crusade against good,
I will feel the emptiness,
and the carelessness inside of me,
I will learn to love it,
I will let it grow,
into what I have become,
a human who does not feel pain only pleasure.
Pleasure of pain.

Paralyzes

Love is an illusion
solitude is an inevitability
feeling a torment in the heart
seeing a tear in the mind
knowing an attack on sanity.

Hope left years ago
dreams flown away
faith is non residing
beliefs atheistic
energies compiled.

Darkness is warm
living in the shadows
light burns my essence
bright cold as ice
monger of pain and suffering.

Sanity to perfection
losing mind to spirit
essence not letting go
left behind reason faith
alone till the end.

Skinless

Fuck the world
Fuck goodness
Fuck liberation
Fuck respect
Fuck everybody.

Why!...............why!.............why?

For being born into this world,
as a cursed kind being,
always running away,
hunted by curses,
never able to escape,
knowing that nothing will ever succeed,
because the curse will never leave.

How can one live in kindness?
and how long will that kindness last,
and what if I cast the good away,
would it not be the salvation?
then a curse would be a blessing,
and it would not be a bad thing,

→

Life is just one state of torment,
waiting with eagerness to exhale,
but that will never happen,
there the curse lies strong,
providing my heart, a great passion,
not allowed to see the light.

Haunted at day by the nightmares at night,
Insomnia for days, months, years,
Standing in darkness for all eternity,
Held only in good by the thread called love,
But the thread is fading rapidly,
Because love does not reside in me anymore.

My mind is slowly drifting,
To the land of insanity,
My heart will soon follow,
Then they become a unity again
Now all I wish and all that is left
Is a straitjacket and exile for rest.

Whispers

An adventure now is done
I'm travelling home again
I feel a little empty inside
like a sad feeling of no more.

Empty inside after so many impressions
like my mind is wind up
and is now calming down
to the cold truth of realism.

Tears are slowly shaping in my eyes
come to say the last goodbye
soon a new era will come
and I will get swallowed up again.

This is the way of a nomad's life
no home, no grounds, no roots,
seen the world in many joys
always in a state of loneliness.

Autumn

Brown threes colouring the scenery
Atomic weather fogging the horizon
Greyish dark enclosing the sun
A mindset of melancholy

Wind shaking the threes violently
Leaves collaring the pavement red
Drizzle making the walkability slippery
Half-hearted decisions emanating within

Cuddling with the blanket of warmth
Enjoying the honey filled hot thee
Reminiscing from the days old
invigorating the years in time

A mosaic potpourri of thoughts
Floating in the cerebral space
Lazy indifferent attitude
Humming body of delight

Brianism

Religion is the man-made belief
Created by the minority to govern the majority
A selfish act of Me and I
This is the power of truth

Priests, cardinals and popes are
The scum of humanity
In the beautiful bosom of justice

A world without religion
Would be a world without war
A world where everybody is equal

The human values are what counts
Not what they belief
Many wars are created in the name of religion
Innocent lives have received
Religious smear of nothingness

The holy grail is sought, sacrificed and butchered
for
Only to find it inside the humans itself
They are values, standards and compassion
The world has an evil called religion

$\longrightarrow$

God does not exist but what exists are
Compassion, justice and love
Helpfulness and mutual respect
But they exist within us if we want them

Man, today walks this earth
Without reflecting it to himself
Some are without, a dying world
The cause is called religion

We are all of the same creed not the same religion
Black, white, red, Muslim, Christian and Jew
We are all one in the history of man
We are all one

Borderline

I feel so alone in this world
no one knows my pain
no one tll1derstands
the emotions inside.

I look for a way out
a scent of hope
an allied in my fight
an emotion of power.

Faith is not optional
I know my curse
energies are my books
I know what is beyond.

I am losing the fight
I cannot overcome anymore
walls I keep hitting
surrendering heart.

Cosmologies

I envy the people of this world
they are blessed with blindness
the divine feeling of not knowing
what lies beyond that cannot be seen.

I feel for truly paranormal humans
for they know a fraction of the beyond
but still even they cannot comprehend
the reel truth of the great black.

This world is a part of a larger symbioses
the greater universe of it all coexisting
one cannot live without the other
dark matter the key consists of life energies.

Watchmen spread all over the universe
walking amongst humans with the knowledge
feeling, knowing, seeing since before the dawn of
man
we are a part of the dark matter the nexus of light.

Mortal envy

In hell everything is hurting.
Quitting life in this world there is nothing left.
Tormented every day, can't do it anymore, am
tired.
Just want to get out, don't belong here anymore.
Haven't even an identity, that was an option never
allowed.
Am tired of all the walls, am tired of nothingness,
no more.

Spreading the last in life and then it's done.
Then this world can go to hell,
cause that's where the world would send you.
An obsolete person in a world where nobody
gives a damn.
Where everybody is busy taking and not giving.

Well don't want to live in that world anymore.
Kindness, goodness are virtues which are
forgotten.
Can't do it anymore, throwing down the fight.
It's too strong to beat, am struggling inward.

Schizoid depression is running through my heart,
insanity is lurking in my brain.
I'm cursed with the ability to feel and see.

Feel and see the pain of others.

Feel and see.........

Dancing heart

Love is like an inferno
You can find warmth in it
Or you can burn yourself
It can be used regardless

Love moves mountains
It gives the power to rise again
The ability to be able to forgive
It can cope the expansion of joy

It can disappear into darkness
Withdraw and hide away
Push everyone away
Boil over and make mistakes

But it will always be there
Like a seed in inner state
It can never be kept down
It shall always prevail

Depth

A world without beauty
Is a world without light
A world without hope
Is a world without life

In hope lies the seed of life
In the light shines' beauty
In life the seed grows strong
Beauty is the nourishment

People often walk in the dark
Not able to see the light
And doing good deeds fade
Or being the deed, itself dies

Find the road that leads to the light
Let it shine and share it with others
Don't be selfish give hope space
Let your strength conquer the darkness

Doomsday

Drones in a heartless society
Enslaved robot-like movements
Optimized work relations
Constructive independence drowned

Mechanical days no deviations
Numb knowledge without expansion
Ambitions yet a statistic money machine
Love a passing of genetic material

Emotions a sign of weakness
None tolerated phenomenon
A devaluation of work powers
Morale another unnecessary cost

Purification of the weak
Camouflaged as a gesture of good
Individual regicide, do to progress
Justice knee'ed by capitalism

Realms

Imagine a world beyond,
a world of soul's pure energy.
Imagine that your dreams transpire from there,
and you will never know but a dream.
Imagine that humans are merely born as a shell,
a host for the soul to live in.
What if our world is the dream world?
and the soul world is the real world.

What happens with a person?
when he has seen, felt and knows,
seen the real world with beautiful eyes,
felt the tranquility it provides,
and seeing the destructiveness in our world.
Suicide, insanity, hatred, addictions.............
And what if that person knows,
No matter what he does, he is doomed to walk the
earth

How does a person comply to that?

Individuals

The sun is shining
Spring is standing on the door threshold
Gathering in the green
Nectar enrich the senses

Opposites tolerate
Love floating in the air
Bodies roused by beauty
Gazes revealing intentions

New alliances emerge
Old ones are renewed
Silliness challenging frowns
Age differences erased in presence

Philosophical debates
Clarify world situations
A bond of being
A togetherness that shines

Recalibrating roads

Melancholic sadness
Remembering what was
Missing the warmth of love
Aching for the sense of touch.

Soul mate lost to the dark
The dark that roams in me
I could not see it in the light
But I saw it in the darkness.

I cannot forgive my self
For the pain I caused the one I love
Solitude is my punishment
Remorse the knife that penetrates my heart.

I walk the streets of life
Without pride or joy anymore
For I will never be with the one
That brought peace in my soul.

Flourishing

Love is the thread of life
Unconditional is the method
Mutual respect must be
Individually but yet as one

Love breeds kindness
Capacity for unselfish acts
A beautiful though can become an ideal
That in time spreads more love

Love can be many things
The love for one's family
Or the love for another
Or merely love itself

Love is the gift we have received
To create paradise on earth
To give for the pleasure of joy
And don't forget the little things

Saint

Silent loneliness
Mathematical precision
Camouflaging pain
Coagulating madness.

Out world spectator
In world insanity
Sieged mind in time
Portal knowledge.

Captured heart
Black as carbon
Shining diamondish
No one will ever know.

Wandering in time
Has seen what was
Knowing what will be
Empathic enlightenment.

Equilibrium

Phone is ringing another assignment
An opportunist has arisen
Kissing the wife and children goodbye
They are the counterpart to the inhume misdeeds

Flying towards a new country and a new face
Informed of the task by my superiors
Finding my settings in the hotel room
I assemble the machine of my livelihood and wait

Across the street a meeting of criminals is held
A meeting that defies humanity
Hours go by, people arrive, meeting is held
The target sits at ease without knowledge of
termination

Take aim with the machine, finding target
A whistling sound occurs
Tearing metal, a shattering window
Blood spraying a whole in the chest

$\rightarrow$

Leaving the machine as I disappear
Confirming with my contact assignment fulfilled
Flying back to a state of normality
Assignment already in the past

Kids hugging me on save return
The wife hugs me with joy in mind
She knows very well the work I do
Retiring guilty that escapes

But demons hunt the mind
Are no different from the others
Working legally for the government
Evil deeds for mankind

Taking comfort in my family
They are the world to me
Phone is ringing a new assignment
A hitman on the side of humanity

Reset

Humans are the virus of death and evasion
Killing the earth with there seeds of devastation
No thought of the outcome of there actions
The earth will not stand for these selfish attractions

A beacon of light
Will slay the human with might
A force of nature will claim
The human filth of shame

The floods will arise
Ridding the earth of human demise
The volcanoes will roar with wrath
Resetting the earth for a new path

There shall be no remorse
Humans already set their course
The rain of man has come to an end
Earth now the lands will defend

Honoured in life

Emerging of love
Existence spectating from within
Small hands touching life
Unique, divine and untouched

Words and rhymes and child laughter
Skipping rope, hula hoops and playful
A schoolyard full of life
She blossoms on the road ahead

True love blossoms along the way
In church she sealed with "I doo"
With a mood of happiness, rice and tin cans
They are sent on the journey of life

Extinguished energies of life
She is graced with time as her companion
Floating towards her last journey
While tears proclaim a great loss

Spiritus naturalis

Feeling the essence of an ending
Torment in time of a single day
Seeing me in a light of craziness
People taking distance from me.

Changing essence in a man
Draining me of my energies
Giving him the power to self heal
Gesture unnoticed by fear.

I have the power of feeling
I feel everyday all day
The doubt the fear the despair
Of the people in this world.

The pain I have of other people
Is a hurting of a thousand years
A fight to keep my goodness
A spirit strongly corrupted by pain.

The Watchmen

On this earth we are but a few
Who protects this world?
From its evil residue
We are a breed, a descendent of crusaders.

We have been fighting in many ages
From ancient Egypt to Vikings and knights
From before, from now and forever after
We are the night breed called the watchmen.

We live in the shadow of light
We see we feel the evil might
We are the protectors of all that is good
Empathy, energies are the weapons we use.

We travel in dimensions we know the truth
Death is not a luxury we can choose
Every watchman that walks upon this earth
Are from before, from now and forever after.

Good morning

Waking up bathed in the light
Birds are chirping lyrically
The night lawn is alluring
In a state of bliss

Parking myself on the terrace
The sun is warming me inside
Birds are inspiring the mood
The lawn seduces the senses

Sitting for a long-time captivating
The many expressions of the morning
Enriched with the views of life
The dew is enchanting the mind

Quietly Enjoying the aroma of the coffee
Processing the impressions stagnation
Leisurely creating duties
Going to work in tranquillity

The covenant of generations

We are a generation
Born from the loins of selfishness
A 70´s mindset
That should have been good

A group without identity
With a background of black holes
And an approach of me first
Created by our parent's newfound free spirits

Our children are the second generation
Of the continuum of our behaviour
A flock of chameleons in this society
Without foundation or empathy

The generation before us tries to rectify
Without consideration of the generations effect
Without thinking of the generations decay
They only cast shadows on a bottomless lake

Token

Cursed in the wonders of life
Living in the darkness of doubt
Fed by the tales of knowing
Persecuted in the state of insanity.

Never a moment of peace
Always on the run
From my heart's instrument
The premonition to see.

Always in a mind of despair
Trying to hope for good
But every time I try to get up
Something always pulls me down.

My last resort in this world
Is to avoid all life
To lock myself in
So, I'll never see in pain again.

The observer

The Clock on the wall is ticking
The teacher is talking about compositions
vaguely hearing it my mind is floating
My thoughts are elsewhere

Next to me she is sitting
The most beautiful I have ever seen
With hair as black as the night is long
And brown eyes that will make you melt

Yesterday just another sweet girl
An accidental incidence occurred that moved focus
A coincidental touch and a long gaze
After class we were sitting close to each other

The heart is racing, and the thoughts are spinning
Does she feel the same
We are so different from two worlds
We are two decades apart

$\rightarrow$

The Clock on the wall is ticking
The teacher is talking about compositions
vaguely hearing it my mind is floating
My thoughts are elsewhere

Next to me he is sitting
The funniest gentleman I know
With the cute light and fluffy hair
With those blue eyes that warms every heart

Yesterday just another good friend
An accidental incidence occurred that opened my
eyes
A coincidental touch and a long gaze
After class we were magically close to each other

Thoughts are spinning and there is a lump in my
heart
Is he overwhelmed with the same feelings
We are so different he is wise in life
Why would he settle for an ignorant youth

$\rightarrow$

The Clock on the wall is ticking
The teacher is talking about compositions
Two people sitting and hearing nothing
They are affected by the incident in the past

They are relishing in their own thoughts
They do not notice the observer
Their worlds collided yesterday
Close proximity is their witness

They sit there with the demons of standards
In their search for answers within
The closeness becomes an insecure distance
They push each other in opposites directions

Suddenly they sit far from each other
Greeting awkwardly every day
They chose like many others to listen to reason
Two on the same emotional plain lost forever

Blinded egos

Hells train is chugging along
Man, blindly boards it
With a mindset of me
They don't know where it ends

Stations scurry along
The visual warning in the window
Man is blindly stuck
In the reflection of the glass

Mutilated and pail bodies
Sitting next to man
In the mixed compartments of the train
The wall of indifference is shadowing all

The end station is in sight
Man discovers the destination
Squeals, excuses and evasiveness
But hell lets no one out

Dawn

The sweet humming of love
Spellbound by the silent whispers
The call of connectedness
The bliss of the soaring hearts

The sparkling touch of warmth
The merging of the souls
The body energy of attraction
The powerful coexistence of love

The golden spectacle of beauty
Beating hearts revealing
The beauty in the eye of the beholder
Eternal bliss

Watching, feeling and adoring
Wishing only to strive for better
The assuring beauty of life
The eternal bosom of gratitude

Human nature

Empty streets
Heavy atmosphere hanging in the air
Silence embracing the illusion
Refusing to be suppressed by righteousness

A boom, a bright light a mushroom cloud in the
horizon
A beautiful sight overpowering the mind
Interrupted by an all-consuming shockwave
Chaos, noise, pain, fading world

Another uncurable scar on mother nature
Another civilisation perished
Victim of the upper hand of progress
Nothing learning, nothing will change

Crowded streets
No chaos, no noise, no pain, fading world
Ignorance in the air, invisible killer
Evolved progress, entrenched attitudes

Primal force

Background noises from the telly
Faded light creating a warm mood
The embracing of love on the couch
Silent humming newfound delight

The pleasure of casual moments
Frozen time living in the moment
Beautiful gazes of acknowledgement
The creation of warm bodies by touch

Two open minds drawn to each other
Have relinquished all insecurities
Letting the duality of life leaching in
The joy of mutual acceptance

Night is unveiling, a school day tomorrow
The abrupt awakening of parting
Had just found the basics of existence
Do not want to relinquish the feeling.

$\longrightarrow$

Two hearts beating untamed
The pull of eternity will not let go
The souls are screaming for more
Heavy steps toward home begins

Fence is reached, scurrying from the door
Hugs and kisses, chatting and recognition
Deciding to experience the night together
Not caring about the ripples that will follow

Alarm clock ringing, a new day
Glowing from infatuation
The ripples are nothing but good
Walking hand in hand no fears

Friendly warmth and smiles
Hugs and joys follow
Have known for a while
The leap was finally taken

Samurai

I am a samurai in this world
It is a part of me and my travels
I will never be anything else
A relic from an ancient past

A ronin I have become
For I am driven without a master
Duty, honour, courage and charity
Are the virtues I fight for

In this era without honour
I wander for whom who will be
With kindness in spirit and soul
For whom justice is out of reach

But all these virtues I fight for
Are often in vain in this world
I am a samurai and often I fight
But in this world, I am an outlander

Trapped

Trapped between the doorways of life and death
Trapped in the emotions of love and hate
Trapped in a world of good and bad
Trapped in a cause of needing and rejecting.

Trapped in a mind of sanity and insanity
Trapped in the illness of mania and depression
Trapped in sight by the world and dimensions
Trapped in the heart by knowing and feeling.

Trapped in life by pain
Trapped on the road to oblivion
Trapped in a state of no hope
Trapped in me.

Haiku

Forever darkness
Thought's travel to nothingness
Non will ever change

Golden moments are
Disappearing loneliness
Eternity's light

Gray travelling clouds
Beyond the black horizon
Destruction lies there

Growing loneliness
Beyond paralysation
Vanishing life signs

I love beyond doubt
I pray for beyond reasons
I see through too much

                    Sudden accident
        Beyond doubt, beyond reason
                    Totally madness

Life is the hard way
Death is the easy way out
Which one do you choose?

                    Everlasting love
        Hearts breaking by timeless sins
                    Eternity is

Eyes meeting halfway
True love is beyond heaven
Everlasting love

Time is innocent
People are the guilty ones
Changing devils' name

Life is damnation
Believing in nothingness
Eternally souls

Fading illusions
Loving destructive powers
Life is damnation

Looking in mirrors
Reflections of nothingness
Surrounding it all

Whispering water
Sweet music of falling tears
Making sad noises

Beautiful flowers
Sun making smiling faces
Love is eternal

Love is together
Madness conspiring feelings
Confusion beyond

Walking cloudlessly
Searching for the piece inside
Never to be found

Shining love scenting
Heart torn, conflicting, stands still
Falling in too deep

Lying on the grass
Looking up on the lost stars
Where did we go wrong?

Betraying friendship
Consuming sadness is hate
Feeling is vengeance

Empty buildings are
Wondering silence within
Never changing path

Betrayal within
He wonders painful on earth
Prophecy foretold

Legacy is birth
Enchanted is decisions
Destiny human

Redemption at hand
Oblivion is living
Defeating mindness

Love is flowing strong
Restless souls searching, needing
Finding attraction

Faith is decided
Or is it what we make it
What do we make true?

Escalating war
Worldwide expanding beyond
Fugitive state none

Choices in making
Decisions made of the heart
No one can escape

Love is devotion
The quest without selfishness
Faith without boundries

Candlelight dinner
Two souls soaring in one space
Eyes shining brightly

Compassion roaming
Purity glowing in heart
rarely in time

chirping birds confirm
sunlight through misty windows
spring has arisen

smell of warm coffee
morning dew caress my face
simple things matter

noises far away
the silence of the country
lifes simplicity

watching from far
the sounds of humming students
warming my essence

roaring thunder is
herold for lightning coming
rain rise of new dawn

running in the rain
washing all the dirt away
fresh start arising

a world torn apart
evil politicians are
greed the ruler is

spinning head inside
conniving little bitches
spawning seeds within

electronic world
destroying humanity
recalibrate now

smartphone wars raging
human being transforming
zombie nation grows

breaking the cycle
evolving to betternes
discarding the world

human caveman is
edge of oblivion neighs
ignorance whispers

Ode to the reader
Hoping satisfaction be
Bidding you farewell

Bonus!!
Lyrics of a Viking

Crazy living fool

I'm walking in a shadow with my fucked-up mind
where do we go and what can we find?
everyone I meet say I look alright
but they can't see how I'm hurting inside
all that I do and all that I am
Is nothing more than a fucked-up man.

I'm living in a world on my fucking own
No one to talk to all alone
Looking now from my point of view
Drugs make you fly that's the right thing to do
and all that I do an all that I find
Is nothing more than a doped-up mind

I'm flying on the edge with my fucking wings
just flying around minding my own things
and one day those wings will surely disappear
and I don't care that means the end is near
And all that I hope and all that I wish
is no more feeling this emptiness

Drugged up reality

When I look into the mirror
and when all that I can see
Is the emptiness in my eyes
And the shadow next to me
I wonder how I got here
and I don't know what to do
and the only thing I can find
is this crazy mind of mine

I live in a reality I made up
the only thing I know is doing drugs
I don't know what happened to me
I was living my life beautifully
I love the clean feeling
Of getting reel high
It makes you feel
like you're so alive

I don't ever think I want to stop
drugs are good and a lot of fun
why be sad -in your life
When you can get happy drugged up
and you have nothing to worry about
cos the only thing that can be
is that your body dies
and that's liberation in my eyes

Clouded minds

When I get up in the morning light.
I look into the mirror with all its fright.
And I don't like what I see,
cos all I see is another me.
And when I see myself in the eyes.
All that I see is emptiness and lies.
And what do you do when there is no hope at all
Just O.D. on drugs, and hope that HE calls.

I see myself with a needle in my arm.
I'm a fool I'm crazy but I do no one harm.
And I don't care what they say,
I'm not here for a pleasant stay.
And when I see myself from above.
I see a death without any love.
And what do you do when all hope is lost.
Just O.D. on drugs and pay the little cost.

Looking outside at people on the street.
I line up on the mirror, my daily mind treats.
And doing that makes me feel.
That my pain inside isn't real.
And when I'm walking all alone.
I realize I'm on my own.
And what do you do when all hope is none
Just O.D. on drugs, and hope you're soon gone.

Sad destiny

When the love inside
is tearing you apart
and the only thing you feel
is an empty lonely heart
Then you have a choice
that you have to make
Will your heart heal?
or will it surely break

As you sit alone
in your empty space
and you wonder why
you long for sweet embrace
Then you have a chance
that you have to take
Will your heart feel
or will it surely ache

And when you're walking down
on the hollow empty places
and the only thing you see
is your life slowly erases
Then you have a chill
that you have to face
Will your heart fill?
or will it surely daze.

Strange love

When I look into your eyes
I like what I see
Cos I see a loving girl
Who wants to be with me.
And all that I know
And all that I care
Is that I love you
Every day and everywhere.

Every time I'm with you
I feel I'm in heaven
And everything you say
Is the right thing?
And all that I despair
And all that I repent
Is that you my love?
Have another boyfriend

I love you with all my heart
I know what to do
But I feel tom apart
Cos I want to be with you.
And all that I do
And all that I feel
Is I can't stop loving you
More and more day by day.

Betrayed world

What is this world we're living in?
Where trust is betrayed by your best friend
We live our lives counting on people
But what do we do in a lifetime?
Where friends sell you out
Whatever happened to loyalty and respect?

And how do we live in a world
Where you are betrayed time after time
How do we keep our trust and faith?
In a life where there is only disrespect
And can we even survive in a place
Where you have no cover of friends.

I've been asking myself that same question
But I haven't been able to find any conclusion
So, ask yourself that question again and again
What would you do living in that world
And never known anything else but betrayal
Would you be able to keep your sanity?

Moneymaker

All that I see is a lot of crime rates
And it's all because of religion and ridiculous race
hate
Whatever happened to protecting laws?
Are the innocent lost to rebels without cause?

Moneymaker, moneymaker, moneymaker
Money makes the world scream loud
Moneymaker, moneymaker, moneymaker
Money makes the world shine proud

Is there a future for registrations?
Or is it just in our imaginations
What could be said and done
To make it a hopeful place for everyone

Moneymaker, moneymaker, moneymaker

All that I see as a lot of time
For gangsters and mobsters to do organized crime
The police have sold the devil their soul
To get on the mobsters very rich payroll

Moneymaker, moneymaker, moneymaker

What can we do to stop these fears?
Of police turning against us in bitter tears
How much money is one life worth?
When will they stop putting money first?

Moneymaker, moneymaker, moneymaker

No more violence

I came into the bank, to cash some money
Two guys came in, they sure looked funny
One drew a gun, the other yelled freeze
They said they'd kill us if we called the police

Stop the violence, freeze the violence
No more violence, fuck the violence

I was going down the street, just looking around
I was looking at a shop when I heard the sound
I felt a sting in my chest, and got very hot
It occurred to me, for no reason I'd been shot

Stop the violence, freeze the violence
No more violence, fuck the violence

I went to a hotel, to get some sleep
I paid a lot of money, it wasn't cheap
The hotel blew up, in the middle of the night
I went to heaven, without even a fight

Stop the violence, freeze the violence
No more violence, fuck the violence

I was at home, sitting in my chair
When a burglar came in, he didn't care
He just drew a gun, and blew me away
I didn't even have, nothing to say

Stop the violence, freeze the violence
No more violence, fuck the violence

I'm sitting in the court, for doing a crime
I was convicted, now I'm doing time
I was not guilty, the judge knew
The mob had threatened, what can you do

Stop the violence, freeze the violence
No more violence, fuck the violence

Unjustified

Here I am walking down the street
looking around for something to see
and all that I see is police brutality
they're stupid and mental and looking for alibis
and if they don't find it, they'll just beat you up
They'll just smash you like a very old cup.

Everywhere you go
and everywhere you look
It's unjustified
It's unjustified

Everywhere you go
and everywhere you look
It's unjustified
It's unjustified

They think they can hide behind their badges
they think they are angels in disguises
they think they can do anything
and get away without a sentence ring
well think again and one more time
there are laws build for different crimes

Everywhere you go

There's no limit to what they'll do
They won't even try to help you
They don't even care if you are guilty or not
They just put you away and lock you up
If that is what the police is today
I have just one damn thing to say

Everywhere you go

Regrets

If I could I would have said the things I want
If I could I would have told you what I've been
going thru
But I couldn't see, I was blinded by hate
But I didn't tell you and now it's too late

I regret I didn't do the only right thing
I'll regret it, till I've become a lonely has been
And of all the regrets that I can find
None of them has, the right time

You left me because you thought I had another
It was my fault you didn't know what was wrong
But now I know, I should have told you the truth
And that is how much, that I love you

I regret I didn't do the only right thing

There is nothing left but the waiting sorrow
I wake up every morning without a tomorrow
Every night when I go to bed
I dream I'm in your arms when I wake

I regret I didn't do the only right thing
I'll regret it, till I've become a lonely has been
And of all the regrets that I can find
None of them has, the right time